Other titles by Roland Sawyer Barth

Improving Schools From Within
Run School Run
Open Education and the American School

CRUISING RULES

Relationships at Sea

ROLAND SAWYER BARTH

Illustrations by Jon Luoma

 HEAD TIDE PRESS

First Edition

ISBN 0-9654467-0-0
Library of Congress Catalog Card Number 96-80123

Published by Head Tide Press, Alna, Maine 04535
Printed by J.S. McCarthy Company, Augusta, Maine

Designed by Joanna Barth

I should be happy!—that was happy
   All day long on the coast of Maine;
I have a need to hold and handle
   Shells and anchors and ships again!

— Edna St. Vincent Millay
from *"Exiled"*

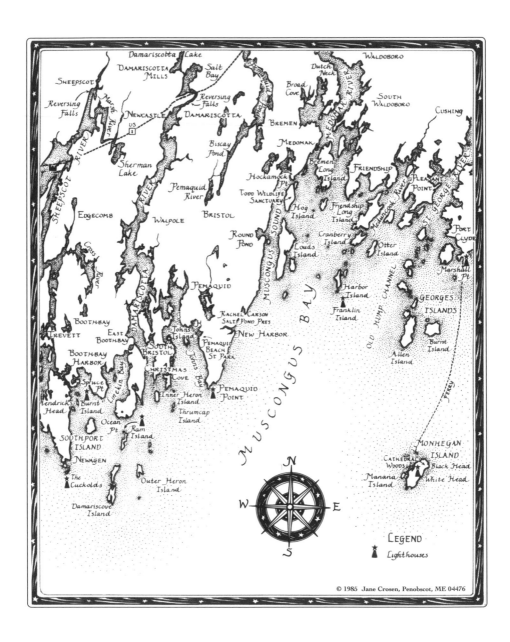

WALDOBORO

DAMARISCOTTA Lake

SHEEPSCOT

DAMARISCOTTA MILLS

Salt Bay

Dutch Neck

Reversing Falls

Broad Cove

SOUTH WALDOBORO

CUSHING

NEWCASTLE

US 1

Reversing Falls

DAMARISCOTTA

BREMEN

MEDOMAK

Sherman Lake

Biscay Pond

Bremen Long Island

FRIENDSHIP

PLEASANT POINT

EDGECOMB

Pemaquid River

Hockamock Pt.

Todd Wildlife Sanctuary

Friendship Long Island

WALPOLE

BRISTOL

Hog Island

Cranberry Island

Otter Island

PORT CLYDE

Round Pond

Louds Island

Marshall Pt.

BOOTHBAY

TREVETT

Rachel Carson Salt Pond Pres.

New Harbor

Harbor Island

Franklin Island

GEORGES ISLANDS

EAST BOOTHBAY

Johns Island

SOUTH BRISTOL

Pemaquid Beach St. Park

BOOTHBAY HARBOR

Burnt Island

CHRISTMAS COVE

Allen Island

Spruce Pt.

Inner Heron Island

Pemaquid Point

MUSCONGUS BAY

Hendrick's Head

Burnt Island

Ocean Pt.

Ram Island

Thrumcap Island

SOUTHPORT ISLAND

NEWAGEN

MONHEGAN ISLAND

The Cuckolds

Outer Heron Island

CATHEDRAL WOODS

Black Head

White Head

Manana Island

Damariscove Island

N
W   E
S

LEGEND

Lighthouses

© 1985 Jane Crosen, Penobscot, ME 04476

Contents

Preface

You are about to encounter the abundant absurdities of life in relationship aboard ship. I have long been fascinated with the art form known as "sailing." I have only recently discovered that there *is* an art form known as "relationship." *Cruising Rules* is a collection of stories about the two art forms together — sailing in relationship, yet a third art form.

Very little in our lives is more important than our relationships with those we care about. And very little is more inscrutable, and problematic — particularly for men. Relationships can be taxing, even toxic.

In order to live in relationship, we need to laugh at ourselves and with one another. We must acknowledge and savor our ridiculous times together. Every interpersonal event — especially the absurd — carries with it important learning. The challenge is to extract, from all the gravel that accompanies our time together, the gold. Laughter, accompanied by analysis, is the panning sieve. The more the mirth and reflection, the more learning; the more the learning, the more our satisfaction together.

It's as simple as that. And as complicated.

"When in doubt — tell the truth," Mark Twain suggested. Well, everything you are about to read is true. Names have not been disguised in order to protect the guilty. It all actually happened — to the best of my recollection. Unfortunately, my recollection of life with others at sea during these many years is a bit blurry. So this is probably not *just* as it was, but rather the way I *remember* it was — a kind of impressionistic painting. Allow me some poetic license in writing, and I shall allow you the same in reading.

The details don't really matter, anyway. What matters is that our experiences carry with them astonishing insights. These stories, aged in my soul's cask over the years, are idiosyncratic, even peculiar. Yet they express metaphors and teachings which are universal and lasting for me — and, I hope, useful for you. They are offered in hopes that each of us may find abundant and buoyant joy in our all-too-brief passages with one another. Welcome aboard!

Alna, Maine   Roland Sawyer Barth
Spring 1998

Acknowledgments

I want to thank all of those who have suffered my company these many years aboard ship and ashore; many wonderful moments in wonderful relationships. And I want, especially, to acknowledge Snyder for germinating with me the concept of "Cruising Rules."

Thanks to many readers of early manuscripts: Audrey, Doreen, Jeff, Jenney, Joe, Paul, and Sarah. Special thanks also to Roy Guyton and Hsueh Yeh for their computer expertise. For their editorial wizardry, I thank Matthew Abbate, Jane Crosen, and Petra Nicholson. My love and respect to my daughter, Joanna, who so elegantly designed this volume. And my great admiration to Jon Luoma, for so artfully converting verbal images into visual ones. Finally, my deep affection and appreciation to Petra for inspiring and assisting me in creating this book.

Setting Sail

Cruise: Two or more days spent continuously on
a boat that is underway, with stops for the night.

— John Rousmaniere
The Annapolis Book of Seamanship

"Roland, are we on Cruising Rules yet?" With these words,
Snyder always comes aboard. Snyder (those who don't know
him call him Robert; to those who *really* don't know him, he is
Bob; to the rest of us, he is simply Snyder) and I owned a
succession of three Friendship sloops—graceful, gaff-rigged,
wooden, turn-of-the-century Maine coastal fishing boats.
Sometimes he and his family sailed together, sometimes my
family and I sailed. But once a year Snyder and I sailed—just
the two of us. We called our brisk Columbus Day cruising
weekend on the coast of Maine "the boys' night on the town."
During our three or four days together, things were different.

For instance, our cuisine. In planning the menu for our first
"night on the town," each of us agreed to bring "some stuff." We
figured the law of averages would yield a balanced, and perhaps
nourishing, diet. Snyder brought a five-pound brick of cheddar
cheese, a case of ale, and two packages of Oreos. I arrived with
a large hunk of Swiss cheese, some beer, and Oreos. The balance
of our meals ranged from cheddar and Swiss, to cheddar or
Swiss, Molson and India Pale Ale, to Molson or India Pale Ale,

chased (and occasionally preceded) by Oreos. Nourishment could be attended to ashore.

And our conversation was different. Snyder and I revel in organic gardening. The more manure to dilute Maine's rocks, the better. When you put seeds in manure with a little soil and add water, you grow zucchini. Big ones. Lots of them. So the

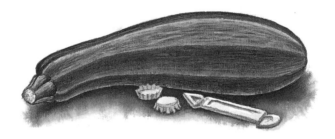

noble zucchini became another companion at mealtime and the centerpiece for many conversations at sea. We once spent an entire evening (over beer, cheese, and Oreos) relating the concept of "friendship" to the fecund zucchini. Consider the endless possibilities: A friend is someone who, when offered a zucchini, will accept it. A friend is one who, when he has an excess of zucchini, will not offer you any. A friend is one who doesn't lock his car during August, so you can load zucchini into the trunk when he isn't looking.

Friendship is a particularly revered quality aboard a Friendship sloop. But mariners know that compatibility on board a sailing vessel is a far more complex and fragile matter than zucchini. No matter how agreeable and adaptable one's partner, there is always the question of "getting along." As our annual adventures began to accumulate, Snyder and I found ourselves running up against the abundant and inevitable warts of the other and even the occasional wart in ourselves. Countless hours living together in a confined, floating space, denied relief by a cold, salty moat, makes things ripe for tension, even conflict.

The first night of one blustery, October cruise found us hunkering down on an anchor in the Davis Cove section of Muscongus Bay, as a gale-force, northwest wind howled above. There we lay Friday night. And Saturday. And Sunday. Plenty of time to get on each other's nerves. On Monday—beer, cheese, Oreos, zucchini, and tolerance depleted—we engined back to Round Pond Harbor, the gale still a-blowin'. I believe it was during these four days of unrelenting intimacy that we promulgated and began to develop the art form that has come to be known as "Cruising Rules."

Laws originate when well-meaning citizens come together to address issues of common concern. From these concerns emerge a set of agreed-upon rules by which humans can live in harmony.

 Cruising Rules are the norms of personal behavior required for two individuals to stay on speaking, even friendly, terms while confined together for an indefinite period in close quarters at sea.

Put bluntly, these Rules determine whether we return to port cordially, angrily, separately, together—or not at all. If Snyder and I were to continue owning and sailing sloop boats together, making mid-course corrections in our shipboard interpersonal behavior was no mere academic exercise.

Snyder and I have refined our Cruising Rules, at first on Friendships, now on other vessels. We have complied with them faithfully, and, I am proud to say on their behalf, we continue to cruise happily together on sea and land alike—fortified, of course, with the now traditional staples of cheese, beer, Oreos, and zucchini.

For a third of a century we have kept these Rules pretty much to ourselves. But a growing realization of their usefulness, even profundity, compels me to place them, now, into the public domain, in hopes they will offer others the same lasting serenity and compatibility on board ship—and perhaps in other leaky relationships—as they have us.

CRUISING RULES

1

The Long Version

Our lives are a trail of un-had conversations. On shore we must speak in code, abbreviation, and haste in the often unsuccessful attempt to get our licks in before the next person intercedes or time expires. Indeed, this is precisely why many of us are forced to use the written word — so we can say *all of it* without interruption.

One of the virtues of being at sea with a companion for an extended passage is the luxury of sufficient time for the "long version" — of everything. "Not that the story need be long, but it will take a long while to make it short" is the way sometime-mariner Henry David Thoreau put it. On a cruise it is possible to experience conversation with leisure, civility, grandeur, and complete resolution.

On the other hand, blessed with a captive audience, and the undisputed floor (or deck), nothing insults and assaults the speaker more than being unceremoniously *interrupted* while attempting the long version. Imagine a preacher delivering an arresting sermon from the pulpit when a member of the congregation stands and interjects a comment, question, or challenge! Hence, the necessity of Cruising Rule 1:

 When a party is talking, he is not to be interrupted until he has completed everything he wants to say.*

We have also found that to be absolutely certain the speaker is indeed finished, a thirty-second interval should be observed at the conclusion of his words before any other party commences speaking.

Sailing vessels are stages for an extraordinary variety of performances: ego podiums. Nothing is so hospitable to a relationship at sea as having a fully attentive, respectful, and silent audience.

*The pronoun "he" is used throughout, deliberately and advisedly.

2

Have I Told You
the One About?

During long periods becalmed, sailing a long tack, or at anchor over beer and cheese, some often tedious, though pragmatic, conversation takes place aboard what the local fishermen call blowboats. "Snyder, while you're below could you get...? Take the helm for awhile, would you? What's the chart say about the depth off of Webber Dry Ledge? See if that's Harbor Island off the port bow."

Occasionally, this discourse is elevated to the realm of "story." We are all, of course, packed to the gunwales with stories ready to be unloaded. So, nothing deflates a relationship at sea as quickly as beginning a promising story, only to have one's companion mutter, "Oh Roland, you told that one on our 1974 cruise through Eggemoggin Reach."

Yet it demeans the storyteller to have to preface every tale with the preamble, "Snyder, have I told you the one about...?" It is, after all, stressful to the aging, overtaxed human mind to

3

remember to whom you have told what and when. The solution to this recurring plight became Cruising Rule 2:

 Any story worth telling is worth telling often.

It reassures and warms the soul to tell your companion any story from your lifelong repertoire at any time and have it received with enraptured enthusiasm, as if heard for the first time.

3

Shootin' the Breeze

Some stories aspire to the lofty status of humor—tales told for the fun of it and the fun in it. The medical profession has much to say about the benevolent qualities of humor. Western medical science has discovered that endorphins, pain-relieving chemicals produced by the brain, are released into the bloodstream when a person laughs. Clearly, laughter has an anesthetic property essential for good health—and for sustaining collective life in close quarters.

But one person's humor can be another's horror. What may be funny to me may be politically incorrect or not funny at all for Snyder. Consequently, the telling of a story or a joke for the purpose of mirth places the narrator in a most vulnerable, even anxious position. When shooting the breeze, the mariner should allow the conversation, like the wind, to take him wherever it goes. Yet nothing so debilitates a relationship at sea as conveying what is an incontrovertibly funny story, only to be greeted by no response, by a critical response, or by a mere shake of the head. Hence Cruising Rule 3:

 A statement, joke, or story offered with the intent of humor shall be responded to with audible, visible, persistent, and above all, authentic laughter.

So, when Snyder takes out his pipe, opens a beer, and clears his throat, it is time for rapt attention. When he begins to speak, and the first glimmer of a smile emerges from beneath his scruffy beard like a signal flag hoisted in the rigging, it is my cue to be ready. As his words roll into laughter, I respond with a timely signal flag of my own—an appropriate guffaw—as we enjoy a fleeting moment of camaraderie. The moment passes like ships at sea, and then we resume watch for the next sighting.

Who cares whether I hear it, get it, or like it!

4

The Fragile Male Ego

Sailors are a competent, authoritative lot whose knowledge base, particularly of sea lore and technical terms, far exceeds that of the power crowd, let alone the landlubber. It should come as no surprise, then, that an impressed audience is essential to sustaining a relationship at sea. Nothing, on the other hand, is more corrosive than having one's wisdom questioned, challenged, or, heaven forbid, corrected. For example:

Roland: "Look at that beautiful Concordia yawl."

Snyder: "Roland, that's a Tahiti ketch."

This is an egregious affront not only to the fragile male ego, but to a lasting friendship as well. Needed is acknowledgment of our unyielding desire to be right, and Cruising Rule 4:

 Any statement made as fact is, in fact, true and is therefore to be accepted as the truth.

Nothing bonds two sailors more than the appreciation by each of the wisdom of the other. So when Snyder studies the spar of a classy old sloop, anchored nearby, and pronounces, "Roland, hasn't she got a fine Park Avenue boom!" my only acceptable response is, "That sure is one fine Park Avenue boom!" Whatever the hell *that* is!

5

Who Am I?

What we wear on the job, out to dinner, or at home often indicates how we want to be seen, or even who we want to become, as well as who we are. Over the years some remarkable costumes have come aboard. For instance, Gordon once rowed out in the dinghy wearing a three-piece suit, holding above his head a fancy silk parasol. Crissman once arrived in a navy blue, double-breasted blazer with regimental striped tie, and a straw boater lashed down. Colorado cowboy Turnbull came aboard in a Stetson and boots. Thankfully, he left his spurs back at the 4-Bar Ranch.

And then there is Michael. This sartorial Iowan shows up for each cruise wearing a baseball cap with "Boar Semen" prominently emblazoned above the brim. Beneath is a week's stubble. Below that, he sports a chin-to-ankle fireman's coat seeking new life after weighty years of service on the back of a Baltimore city firefighter. Heavy metal clasps and fireproof fabric, in addition to virtually eliminating mobility, make it certain that, should this garment ever fall overboard (with or without its occupant), it will descend to Davy Jones' locker in record time! Emerging from beneath this peculiar foulweather gear is a pair of 1940s seedy, red, high-topped sneakers rescued from Marty's cabin where they were found, on Marty—a few days after his death. "Michael's dead man's clothes," his wife calls them.

On my part, clothing is strictly practical. What I wear on the boat is at the bottom of a descending food chain of increasingly tattered apparel chronically recycled, but never quite discarded. I wear my "good" pants and shirts in polite society. When they become "tendah" (as they say Down East), they are remanded to the farm where they serve dedicated years shoveling manure, planting onions, and tinkering with tractors. When worn knees

and elbows no longer offer protection from the marauding spring black flies, the clothes have exhausted their agrarian usefulness and are mercifully transported to sea, where there are no black flies, to enjoy their last incarnation as "apparel." Thereafter, they assume a final lifetime as rags, useful for cleaning up after a mackerel catch. Thence, an honorable burial at sea.

On a passage, what we wear is also who we are—at the moment, that is. Fisherman, farmer, doctor, lawyer, fireman, chef, professor, athlete, yachtsman—and therein lies the rub. For all of the familiar, reassuring, and hallowed traditions of our nights on the town, Snyder and I frequently show up for a cruise with a new garment, awaiting sea trial. What we are doing, of course, is trying on a new "me." There is, needless to say, considerable vulnerability and risk attendant to trying on anything new, let alone a new persona.

After one excruciatingly long winter during which the need for boats was fulfilled by only an occasional perusal of marine mail order catalogs, I arrived for a cruise with a new and, I thought, particularly "salty" sou'wester, the kind of headgear that only a real Newfoundlander or perhaps Gloucester handline fisherman might don. At the first hint of moisture in the air, I went below and emerged from the companionway thus attired, only to have Snyder greet me with, "Roland, where the hell did you get that ridiculous hat?" I suddenly came in touch with what some members of the male species now call "a feeling," a hurt feeling. After determining there was no intent of humor and after discussing my wounds and identity crisis (the long version), we decided to institute Cruising Rule 5:

Whoever you show up for a cruise as is who you are, and you are to be received accordingly.

So, when Snyder subsequently returned from a trip to Holland and, the very first morning of a "boys' night on the town," self-consciously unveiled a new, black, shiny-visored Dutch sea captain's cap bordered in braid (rather pretentious, I thought), my immediate, mandatory, and only possible response could be, "Mornin', Captain — Sir."

13

6

Steer Clear

I soon learned that not quite all shipboard conversation is to be allowed completion, is funny, is worth telling, or is true. I also found out that one cannot always be who he is.

East wind today. West wind coming up. A long-married couple and I decided upon a modest, three-day cruise from Muscongus Bay to Casco Bay, and back. Early in the cruise, I began to talk about a book I'd recently read on the topic of anger. Before I knew it, we were examining what causes each of us to become angry—and how we express it (or don't). And, before we knew it, we were angry discussing our anger! As more and more flotsam and jetsam from the past began to bob to the surface, storm warnings flew. Recognizing that this was only the morning of day one, with two more days together, we had no difficulty securing a majority vote to switch topics.

Politics. Bad choice. Republicans and Democrats on board soon became embroiled in the tobacco industry, the environment, and taxes. Suddenly new fault lines emerged. Should tobacco (or any industry) be regulated? If capital gains taxes were reduced, just *who* would pocket the money? Should the Maine nuclear power plant be closed? For that matter, is nuclear power good for the environment? Does the ACLU really protect individual rights, or trample on the rights of the majority?

Three long-standing friendships began to unravel. Again. Somehow we had shifted back to anger, and it was still only day one. Days two and three were beginning to look bleak.

Then, suddenly, thankfully, out of the fray, like a welcome glow from Seguin Light, emerged Cruising Rule 6:

 Non-discussibles may be discussed only within swimming distance of home port.

The implications are clear. Cruising people, upon coming aboard, must immediately take inventory of all potentially contentious and therefore hazardous issues. Such as politics, money, religion, family, feelings, sex, relationships...and anger.

All of these must be declared off limits. A vigilant watch must be maintained lest other controversial topics sneak in.

Once the juicy topics are edited from our time together, it may seem little is left to talk about. But as the three of us discovered, now peacefully sailing across the mouths of the Damariscotta, Sheepscot, and Kennebec rivers, a rather generous list of permissible and safe topics remains. Weather: wind, no wind; rain, no rain; fog, no fog. Food: what to eat, when to eat, where to eat, and who will prepare for and clean up after the eating.

Landmarks: Christmas Cove or Damariscove; the Cuckolds or Ram Island? Water: how cold is it? tide coming in or going out? how strong is the current? how steep are the waves? And other vessels: pretty, ugly, classy, tacky, 'glass, wood? And, of course, lobster pot buoys: "God, there are a lot of them!"; colors, strategies for avoiding them, and their use as navigation aids.

The British were not the world's greatest sea power for nothing. They had it right: decorum, taste, and good breeding at all times, especially when facing imminent danger. Their success during naval battle was attributed to their unyielding avoidance of interpersonal battle.

We discovered, on our little cruise, topics and conversations aboard a sailing ship which are safe, produce no anxiety, and cause no risk or damage to those on board. Limiting ourselves to these ensures the tranquil passage of many nautical miles—and days two and three. All other conversation must wait until just moments before the cruise is over—when we can afford to live with the fallout.

7

The Hand That
Holds the Paintbrush

In order to purchase our first Friendship sloop, Snyder and I put together a syndicate of five owners, who collectively put up $2,500 for *Amos Swann*. She was a 26-foot, homely, leaky, and lovable little craft. With her came corroded fastenings, rotten garboards, and two well-worn pumps. And a 1924 Palmer make-or-break engine which required ten minutes to prime, choke, kick the flywheel (with an old rubber boot carried for the occasion), and, if you were lucky, start.

Our plan was to minimize not only our capital outlay but our maintenance expenses as well. So, all of us agreed to assemble at the boatyard each spring to scrape, sand, and paint. Invitations were sent out and commitments secured. When the appointed May weekend arrived—cold, raw, and spitting snow—only two of us arrived with it. So, Snyder and I scraped and sanded. Sunday morning, with *Amos* all primed and ready to paint, we faced a crucial decision: what color should the house roof be?

The arguments were between a clean white, an off-white, battleship gray, and what Snyder, for some mysterious reason, called "cat's-ass brindle." The latter—a brownish, orangeish, somewhat pukish buff, allegedly the authentic hue of the original Friendship sloop—probably evolved as a camouflage for fish entrails, lobster bait, and seaweed. We selected and applied, of course, the brindle.

The two of us, having diligently dispatched our boatyard duties for the fitting-out season, drove home with a feeling of considerable satisfaction, even virtue. This warm aura persisted until, one by one, the other three owners weighed in with their outrage over the dubious aesthetic properties of cat's-ass brindle as the proper topping for *their* boat.

A new rule emerged in time to save the day, the partnership, and the cat's-ass brindle. Cruising Rule 7:

 The hand that holds the paintbrush determines the color.

Only recently did I hear the shoreside version in a school faculty room: "If you choose not to join the committee, you forfeit your bitching rights."

The following year we decided to pay the boatyard to scrape, sand, and paint.

8

Whatever Floats
Your Boat

The spring after *Amos Swann* finished dead last of fifty-four boats in the sloop races in Friendship—and nearly sank crossing the finish line—we sailed our second Friendship sloop down to Maine. Purchased in Massachusetts by a reconstructed consortium, *Moses Swann* was related to *Amos* in name only, neither to be confused with the Swan Boats of the Boston Public Garden. *Moses*, duly named and christened by my father (something of an Old Testament prophet himself), was younger, larger, and faster than *Amos*—despite an ugly propeller which extruded from the port buttock at a decidedly awkward angle. The other end of the shaft was attached to a rusty and unreliable gasoline engine, installed well after she was constructed in 1914.

It had been a beautiful sail from Swampscott—another leg of *Moses Swann*'s maiden voyage. A fresh sou'westerly had deposited us at the mouth of the York River, well into Maine waters. As the sun set, Donald, a new owner and expert sailor, and I furled

the ample mainsail. We learned from a passing lobsterman that
the village of York Harbor was upstream a mile or two. We
motored against the ebbing tide, hailed a local fisherman, and
inquired about a heavy mooring for the night in the swift river.
He pointed out a vacant buoy in the lee of Stage Neck and
assured us it was attached to two thousand pounds of granite.
We led the hefty nylon pennant up over the chock, halfway
out the bowsprit, and to the bitt on the foredeck. Thus secured,
we went below to prepare and enjoy a serious zucchini-and-
cheese casserole. After congratulating ourselves on the day's
passage, we fell asleep, comforted by a gentle breeze and the
secure mooring.

Sometime in the middle of the very dark night, we were
abruptly roused by an ominous jolt. Leaping to our bare feet,
and after depositing generous pieces of scalp on the cabin timbers
overhead, we peered out the starboard portholes. To our dismay,
we beheld a very large, very fancy motoryacht pummeling our
defenseless vessel as a good breeze began to build. Full of indig-
nant anger, we shot up the companionway to hail its sleeping
and derelict crew. We immediately fell flat onto the deck, which
was sloping forward at a cataclysmic angle. We crept cautiously
and uncomprehendingly down the incline to discover, to our
horror, that the entire bowsprit—and a good section of the
bow—were below water. Turning aft, the stern confronted us
like the tail of a bottom-feeding duck.

With all the perspicacity and analytical skills that only two
groggy, off-duty professors could summon, we surmised that it
was *we* who were adrift, now passing the first yacht and about

to collide with a second—still secured to our reliable mooring. We deduced that *Moses Swann*, in the lunar tide, had lifted the mooring off of its familiar home in the mud and was now attempting to transport this pendulum to a new location across York Harbor. The pennant had been too short to extend from the mooring over the bowsprit to the samson post on deck. The tide had been too high. And we had been too innocent to foresee this physical impossibility.

Then we heard the water—seawater—trickling through the ill-fitting forward hatch and anchor hawsepipe. Were we sinking? What to do? Two thousand pounds of strain made it impossible to release the mooring, and a knife to the pennant would make some York Harbor fisherman very unhappy.

In the pitch darkness, we donned life jackets and prepared our dinghy (now lifeboat) with essentials—a gallon of fresh water and two wallets. Deciding that shallow water was preferable to deep if *Moses Swann* was going down, we turned to the engine—which, uncharacteristically, started like a thoroughbred—only to discover the propeller singing merrily in the air in the otherwise silent night. This was a situation for which our beginning Power Squadron course had left us unprepared. Maybe the advanced course?

Fortunately, the tide swept us toward yet another yacht tied up for the night against the wharf. Jumping aboard her, we managed, by flashlight, to secure *Moses* alongside and step off.

We pumped and maintained a "watch" (the meaning of which has never been clearer) for the rest of the night. By morning the tide was out, the mooring stone was becoming accustomed to its

new latitude and longitude, and the bow had reemerged from the brine.

We had plenty of time during those wee hours to ponder the meaning of it all. Initial thoughts were of liability. Who was "at fault" here? Certainly not the yacht we collided with, which awakened us; nor *Moses* who delivered us safely; nor the fisherman who offered the mooring; nor the weighty stone, which could have been weightier. Finally, after holding a brief faculty meeting, it was decided that this unfortunate incident could not have been *our* fault.

Upon deeper reflection, Cruising Rule 8 was born that dark night in York Harbor, Maine, amidst the mud, granite, nylon, wood, and water:

 That which secures us may also sink us.

The meeting was adjourned with the resolution that we had just experienced what marine insurance policies refer to as "an Act of God."

9

Good Though

Next to sinking, nothing can make or break a cruise like eating. Food. Planning, anticipating and savoring the next meal usually commences before the consumption of the current one. Sometimes there is a cook on board, occasionally a chef. But on most cruises, especially among males, there is a dramatically unfavorable ratio between the eager producers and eager consumers of fine meals.

Aboard ship, all of this is complicated by the unavailability of additional staples. The givens in the ship's locker lead to some rather peculiar meals late in a cruise — like mustard and cheese on moldy bread.

Donald, although a distinguished academic and superb sailor, experiences difficulty boiling a zucchini. As we were leaving York Harbor, he prepared a rather unusual luncheon which met with my thinly disguised disapproval. Whereupon, he told me a timely story about two bachelors who enjoyed fine cuisine.

Unfortunately, neither had much skill in preparing it.

Constant complaining about one another's cooking had placed their relationship at risk. In desperation, they devised a rule: "Whoever complains about a meal prepared by the other shall cook all meals for a week." One of the pair, wanting to be relinquished from cooking duties, devised an ingenious plot. He stopped in the park on the way home and scooped up off the curb some recent dog leavings. When he got home, it being *his* turn to cook, he prepared a fine soufflé which included this unusual ingredient, hoping the response from his roommate would yield many cooking-free days. The roommate, upon taking a large bite, turned his face down and his nose up and with both accuracy and tact uttered, "This soufflé tastes like shit — good though!"

This story led inexorably to Cruising Rule 9:

 Whatever is cooked by someone else is to be received, savored, and celebrated with the words "Good though!"

These days on our cruises, scrumptious cuisine emerges from the galley which includes zucchini a la veal Oscar — without the veal and Oscar. And steamy cheese tortellini — without the tortellini. And lobster thermidor — without the lobster. Followed by a liberal dash of frosty Ben & Jerry's Oreo Cookie ice cream — without the ice cream. All prepared and consumed with impunity and immunity. "Good though!"

10

The Town Fathers

Soon after departing York Harbor, Donald went ashore and Snyder came aboard. With the aid of an excellent Esso gas station map, Snyder and I successfully navigated our way somewhere near Cape Elizabeth, and put in for the night. I usually prefer a mooring—but after the night in York Harbor, an anchor offered greater peace of mind. I paddled ashore to inquire of our location and to search for some charts of the Maine coast. This journey was effected on my inflated air mattress, because we had lost the dinghy at sea. The mattress had also performed well the night before on top of my sleeping bag, keeping out the rainwater which paused only briefly on the leaky deck.

Now certain of our location, and provisioned with proper charts, we set sail across Casco Bay. Our intended landfall was Potts Harbor on Harpswell Neck. Diligently following our compass, prudently installed directly over the decidedly ferrous gasoline engine, we attempted to relate its numbers to those of the compass rose on the chart. But why was one compass rose superimposed on another? The Esso map didn't have any! As we approached the east side of Casco Bay, the sun began to set. But we could see well enough to carefully match each of the many land masses before us with each of the many symbols for

land masses on the chart. Perfect! We knew where we were. As we closed on the shore, the clues on the chart remained congruent with the reality before us—all but two. One navigation aid, N-4, appeared off our bow yet showed nowhere on the chart. Conversely, one navigation aid on the chart, R-2, was nowhere to be found with the binoculars.

Undeterred, and convinced we were where we thought we were—and more importantly where we *wanted* to be—we contemplated an explanation. After due deliberation we decided that the resourceful Town Fathers, in their inexplicable and ornery wisdom, had defied the Coast Guard and hauled R-2, probably to sell to a tourist, and had replaced it with N-4, probably surplus World War II stock they had kicking around. In the absence of any dissenting voices, our theory offered persuasive credibility.

Having dispatched these minor discrepancies to our satisfaction, we entered the harbor, neatly missing all of the ominous underwater rocks marked on the chart (the Esso map was both easier to use and created less anxiety). We tied up smartly at the dock beside a lobster boat and congratulated ourselves on successfully completing another leg of our voyage Down East.

It was only then that the huge sign over the fishermen's co-op came to our attention. It announced that we had arrived safely not at Potts Harbor but at Mackerel Cove, some two miles and two peninsulas to the south.

In subsequent years, we have had occasion to question the presence, the absence, and the numbering system of navigation aids along the Maine coast which were not where or what they were supposed to be. And always we find comfort in attributing the discrepancies between what we see and what we should be seeing to the work of the Town Fathers, who, like gremlins, never rest.

The good news is that as the years pass, we are no longer quite so certain the Town Fathers Theory holds (deep) water;

the bad news is that what the chart says *should* be there and what we observe *is* there continues to differ at alarming times and in alarming ways. Fortunately, always offering comfort has been Cruising Rule 10:

 The gods protect beginning sailors and fools—sometimes both at once.

Recently, I asked a distinguished, well-attired yachtsman aboard a distinguished, well-traveled 40-foot sloop his "local knowledge" on passing safely through Bracketts Channel between Job Island and Islesboro. A solitary unmarked rock, two feet below mean low tide appears on the chart—and probably in the passage.

"You simply line up the dock with Tumbledown Dick Point, hoist all sails, crank up your engine to full throttle, shut off your depthfinder, and proceed at hull speed. *I've* never had any trouble," he advised soberly.

Clearly, the gods protect others as well.

11

Held Harmless

Sailing involves an unending array of unexpected events, circumstances, and maneuvers which challenge the ability, resourcefulness, and judgment of the best. It is not uncommon, when the skill of the sailor comes up against the demands of the situation, for something aboard the vessel to break. Nothing is so destructive to the spirit of the mariner and to his relationship with his sailing companion as being held responsible, even blamed, for the damage. After all, the Fragile Male Ego is never more at-risk than while in the company of another male. At the very least, conversation should always delicately consider whether the fault lies with human error or with a structural weakness.

Late one October, Snyder, his Coast Guardsman friend, and I were sailing *Moses Swann* around Pemaquid Point and up the Damariscotta River to be hauled for the winter. It was our last available weekend: Gotta do it. Unfortunately, the appointed

weekend brought with it gale-force winds and treacherous seas.

Well offshore, *Moses* opened up some seams and began to take on water, a lot of green water. At first, the electric bilge pump maintained the balance of inflow with outflow. When the water in the bilge reached the battery, the Coast Guardsman was assigned to the manual guinea pump in the cockpit. When the water began gaining on us again, I went below with a bucket while Snyder, at the helm, tried to hold course.

Despite our heroic efforts, water continued to come in faster than we could bail it out. "That's the definition of sinking!" observed our guest from the United States Coast Guard, dryly.

Well off of Outer Heron Island and headed for Ireland, with engine swamped, battery under, and unable to come about in the gale, I decided to gybe the huge mainsail of *Moses Swann*. The resulting cataclysm fractured the gaff jaws, parted the main throat halyard, and snapped the gaff in two. Ah yes, as the saying goes, "That which does not destroy us makes us stronger."

How heartening, therefore, to hear from my sailing partner that windy day on Muscongus Bay, "You know Roland, these old wooden gaff rigs just don't hold up in a gybe. I guess that's why the world switched over to the Marconi rig." Now *that* is the stuff of a lasting relationship, and an excellent predictor that (once the damage is repaired) another "boys' night on the town" will take place. And therein lies Cruising Rule 11:

 Any damage incurred by a vessel, including fitting out at the boatyard, is due to a deficiency in the equipment and not to the judgment or competence of the individual involved.

Moses limped back into New Harbor, whereupon a freshly installed battery powered the pump once again, emitting a comforting hum all night long. Nevertheless, we slept with arms draped into the bilge as water detectors—just in case.

12

The Comfort Factor

For too many years, sailing, for us, meant not only doing it, doing all of it, but overdoing all of it. We virile males pushed and horsed vessel, crew, guests, and ourselves not only to their full capabilities, but also well beyond until something physical or interpersonal broke. "Testing the limits," I believe counselors of adolescents call it.

When we got our first sloop, we noticed that the mainsail was adorned with three rows of rather quaint pieces of rope. It took us several seasons to learn what they did…and it took another season to learn how to do it. It took even more to actually do it.

We learned that these pieces of rope are called reef points. On a sailboat, as in a car, it is possible to adjust the power according to conditions. The prudent sailor would no more try to sail through heavy winds with full sail up than a sensible driver would move through heavy traffic with full throttle down.

The three sets of reef points enable a vessel to shorten sail and be appropriately suited to roughly 20, 30, or 40 knots of wind. Otherwise, you ship lots of water over the side and/or break something. If that happens, both vessel and relationships may be severely damaged.

Only once have I ever set out with a triple reef. That was when David came from Alaska for his first (and thus far, only) sail on the Maine coast. Unfortunately, his one available October day found it blowing a gale. Therefore, we set out.

Suddenly, we found ourselves in the midst of a snow squall. We struggled to find Round Pond in the approaching darkness—a simultaneous whiteout and blackout. Once we located the harbor, we had to locate the considerably smaller mooring. Just as David found the mooring, the prop found the pennant. "Oh dear," I said politely. To unwind the mess, I dove, naked as a jaybird, from the white deck into the whitecaps. I have not employed three reefs since.

It was only after two decades of living in this state of arrested development—cruising with too much sail up, too little ballast down, too much seawater over the gunwales and into the cockpit, too many numbing rainy days, too much terrifying fog, too many broken gaff jaws, and too many rough passages accompanied by too much lunch lost overboard—that we made an important discovery: One can deliberately choose to avoid excess. It is possible not to subject self, others, and vessel to the punishing, brutal, uncomfortable, and unsafe experiences which lie in endless supply offshore.

It was then we discovered a New World which forever transformed our lives at sea. We had landed upon what is now known as the "Comfort Factor."

At first, of course, this was a discovery made in the names of women and children. While others reveled in the new order, we men merely tolerated sanity at sea. But now, when faced with a decision about whether to set out, to stay out, to motor rather than sail, to reef, to hang it up for the day at cocktail hour rather than groping in the dark, we have begun to hear ourselves say, "Let's consider the Comfort Factor." By doing so we have enshrined Cruising Rule 12:

 Reef early and often.

It has dawned on us that a version of the Boston ward heeler's political advice — "Vote early and often" — may also be good nautical advice. At sea, you can't control the winds, but you can control the sails.

13

Loose Lips

Shortly after the near sinking with *Moses Swann* (but completely unrelated to it) and in deference to the Comfort Factor, we formed yet a third syndicate and purchased a rebuilt, 1911, 35-foot original Friendship sloop. She had the graceful lines of a swan, but not the name. Neither deck nor hull leaked; her diesel engine worked; and she was already handsomely attired in cat's-ass brindle. A twenty-year love affair had begun.

The story went that her name derived from the alcoholic habits of an owner in the '30s who was partial to a high-octane, New Orleans blended whisky. Each summer, he imported a case to accompany him on his foggy cruises. One day a friend nailed to the transom a slat from that case with the word "Sazerac" branded on it. *Sazerac* she has been ever since.

On a bright, spring day *Sazerac* was launched, freshly painted, oiled, and varnished by Paul Bryant's capable hands. She looked like a million dollars. Three of us—Snyder, me, and another owner, who shall remain nameless—sailed her up Muscongus Sound to Round Pond. Now, there are only two submerged impediments between Pemaquid Point and Round Pond. Poland North Ledge, waiting patiently just below water level, and prominently marked by a large can buoy, is one of them.

On that fateful day, when the wind died, the third owner started the engine, took the helm, and powered us along at six knots—all the while engrossed in his own erudite lecture on the sinking of the *Lusitania*. Snyder and I went forward to furl the generous mainsail. Suddenly, the Comfort Factor and our cushioned world of the sea were rudely replaced by an 8.2 Richter-scale jolt. As upper fillings fell to the deck, *Sazerac* lurched over on her beam and ground to an indelicate halt—square atop Poland North Ledge. Neither proper chart nor Esso map were anywhere to be found. Bright green C-3

glistened not ten yards away. "Right, red, return," indeed!
Necessity called upon us to immediately craft Cruising Rule 13:

 Loose lips sink egos.

We agreed that in the rare event damage to the craft is sustained due to undeniably and inescapably human error, lack of
judgment, or just plain stupidity, no discussion of the incident by
those who witnessed it shall occur at the time, or thereafter.
Most especially, nothing will ever be disclosed to those ashore.

The rock has since been locally renamed "_____ Mistake"
in honor of that hapless helmsperson. His identity remains
anonymous despite the fact that the other owners, upon reading
these Rules, have threatened a class-action suit, calling for full
disclosure of his name lest they be mistaken for their errant
(now former) partner.

14

Fatal Attraction

Boats accumulate stuff. Lots of it. Understandably. For, when you are in the middle of the ocean, desperately in need of a piece of equipment—a rigging knife, a socket wrench, an alternator belt, toilet paper—it had better be on board. Yet somehow, something is always missing. Therefore, skippers maintain lists of those items so they may be added to the ship's provisions when next ashore. In this way, the amount of stuff expands to fill—and exceed—the amount of space allotted for its storage.

Aboard ship, an infinite number of pieces of equipment constantly challenge the very finite number of spaces. Thus, a sailing vessel becomes a floating closet which carefully holds a variety of equipment used only occasionally, if at all. It's no wonder the area below is referred to as "the hold." Lockers, shelves, cupboards, lazarettes, cabinets, and compartments are built to conform to peculiar hull shapes and sizes. Into these are stored things of congruent, peculiar shapes and sizes. Every skipper, therefore, must be severe, selective, and yet prescient about what comes aboard. Anything allowed to make the trip from dock to deck must have a clear purpose.

On a sailing vessel, for some curious reason, the vast majority of equipment stowed above and below deck is heavier than water. Put differently: it sinks. On my boat only two pieces of equipment are deliberately designed for this—the leadline and the anchor. And both are best, but not always, deployed when attached to a cleat. Only one piece of equipment seems to have been deliberately designed to float—the life preserver—although we used to carry some old ones used as fenders that did sink. To be completely honest, a zucchini also does float—barely. But I'm not sure it was deliberately designed to. However, by some perverted law of nature and Neptune, the rest seems inexplicably drawn to the sea bottom.

Day or night, under sail or power, at anchor or moored, a magically magnetic force seems to constantly beckon the contents of my floating closet, inviting them to leave their safe, dry, warm nesting grounds and to enter the wet, cold, and unknown ocean. I call it the "Fatal Attraction."

Unfortunately, as all sailors know, quite frequently these non-buoyant pieces of gear don't just abandon ship, they help-lessly succumb to what my gastrointestinal physician calls a "sense of urgency." They leap joyfully over the side.

Take prescription sunglasses. The mooring stone in Round Pond is sprinkled liberally with expensive, carefully ground optical wear, which sprung from my nose into the waters below as I lunged for the buoy, amidst flogging jib and lurching sea.

Then, of course, there are the tools—socket wrenches, sockets, pliers, crescent wrenches—used to service the outboard, remove a cotter pin, repair an oarlock. Usually midway through any project (never upon its completion) the tool, with a mind of its own, decides that it would prefer life at the bottom, rather than the top, of the sea. I remember one night the veritable joy with which my new waterproof flashlight jumped from my grasp as it beautifully illuminated the anchor rode. It then slowly and gracefully twirled through the water, offering an eerie light and watery pirouette all the way down. Its lifetime Eveready batteries no doubt continue to brighten some lobster's lair.

And clothing. How many hats, gloves, shirts, and towels have caught a good puff and leapt overboard? I remember my daughter Carolyn's new red shorts which went directly from ship's locker to Davy Jones' locker, without even pausing on my daughter. Only the apparel which I deliberately and finally *choose* to discard seems to float!

And, of course, there is the silverware. When one is washing dishes in the cockpit, usually after supper in the dark, the last remnants of the dirty, soapy water are happily dispatched over the side. No matter how carefully the bucket of dishwater is inspected, it always seems to contain eating implements. We have now learned to be content with forgettable American Airlines forks and spoons which my resourceful mother liberated from a 727 years ago.

And there is that piece of nautical gear, never found on a proper Friendship sloop, but with which I have recently become acquainted—the winch handle. I've seen "floating winch handles" advertised, but I've never seen one of my winch handles float. When urgently shifted from port to starboard to crank the unruly jibsheet, they literally spring from the hand's tightened grip and execute perfect one-and-one-half gainers into the briny pool.

Snyder and I speculate that if the plug on Muscongus Bay were pulled and the water drained, an extraordinary sedimentary deposit would be revealed: wrenches, winch handles, spoons, forks, eyeglasses, caps, gloves, shoes, towels, nuts, bolts, iron, copper, brass, and stainless from every seagoing vessel since Captain John Smith's best astrolabe abandoned ship in 1605. Enough stuff to handsomely equip every boat on the coast of Maine, we figure.

For years we fought a losing battle. We tried to restrain these magnetic urges. Straps on glasses, binoculars, hand-bearing compass; lines, lanyards, and pennants (even buoyed pennants on endangered crescent wrenches) were to no avail. The more we worried about dropping a screwdriver overboard while at work on the transom rubrail, the more precautions taken not to lose the only brass pin while out on the bowsprit hooking up the forestay, the more tightly our teeth grasped cotter pins, the more certain became their inevitable, irreversible seaward trajectory.

These many losses overboard have also caused unbelievable stress to onboard relationships. I remember once under sail when my daughter's boyfriend dropped a piece of the ship's "finest" dinnerware overboard. This caused some palpable, if unstated, stress aboard. Miraculously, the bowl floated. As we made a pass to retrieve the precious object, the young man grabbed for, touched, and sank it. This unfortunate casualty caused some now-stated stress among all permutations of father, boyfriend, and daughter. It is at such times that human bodies have come close to following equipment overboard. That was, until the gods revealed Cruising Rule 14:

 The rightful resting place for every piece of equipment on board is at the bottom of the sea.

It has now dawned on us that the reason most of the ship's stuff sinks is that it belongs *down* there, every bit as much as the cod and haddock, just as birds fly because they belong *up* there. It is their natural habitat. Life of the ship's gear aboard is aberrant and ephemeral, each item awaiting its earliest opportunity to go home.

We no longer begrudge the winch handle its rightful home. Its true purpose in life is to lounge in the dark mud, beneath eight fathoms of seawater, not work in the glare atop a chrome winch head. We have no business, no right, preventing it from going home. It *will* go home, anyway.

Since we ceased cleverly clasping the crescent wrench, since I stopped worrying about depositing yet another $100 pair of glasses atop the mooring, since we stopped anxiously masticating cotter pins, less seems to have fallen or jumped overboard. Not even the rusting American Airlines spoons. I wish they would.

15

Don't Rock the Boat

I've never had much luck fishing, but this hasn't deterred my everlasting hopefulness and the fantasies which accompany putting on the fisherman's hat. Despite the perils inherent in mixing hooks, lines, and sinkers with mainsheets, jibsheets, and staysail sheets, I have mounted several memorable fishing expeditions under sail.

One drama searching for groundfish was cast off Pumpkin Ledge. Albert, the most passionate and accomplished fisherman known to me, and no doubt to fish, hooked onto a Big One and fought courageously for an hour, only to discover our huge cod was a modest lobster trap. Later that day, lowering our aspirations, we switched to mackerel. We chased a school into Browns Cove and soon loaded up a mackerel rig with five very live ones. Unfortunately, as they came over the gunwale, the line snapped and we parted company. Off they went, in perfect synchrony. "The Rockettes," Albert observed, ruefully.

Another occasion, however, stands out from the rest. Not one, but two Big Ones were boated. Sort of. Co-owner Alan and I set out on a serious bluefish quest. We had heard they were feeding in Muscongus Bay, and were determined to get our share. After a quiet night at anchor near Burnt Island, we arose with the morning light, an incoming tide, and a light breeze. Optimistically trolling two squid-like lures on fifty-pound tackle, we rounded Old Woman Ledge. Suddenly Alan yelled, "I've got one!" And he did. As his pole doubled over and he strained to hang on, I tried to luff up. At that instant, *I* got one! I immediately experienced a deficit of hands and feet, as I did my ineffectual best to attend to Alan, throw off the sheets, grab the helm, hang onto my fishing rod, reel in, and maintain contact with a now severely canted, pitching deck.

Our quarry crisscrossed in *Sazerac*'s wake, and found and fouled one another several yards astern. The sloop, without helmsman or crew, came about, gybed, luffed, ran, and went through its entire repertoire of points of sail as it tried to shake off the two bluefish—and the two blue fishermen. Somehow, we held onto the rods, the rods held onto the fish, and *Sazerac* held onto us all. With yet another hand, we brought the dinghy, *Jedediah*, up hard against the transom, and together reeled the tangled, turbulent rat's nest of lures, lines, and fish alongside—and up and into the dinghy. Squinting through tears of laughter, we observed two thrashingly handsome twenty-plus-pound blues. We gasped for breath—all four of us. The excitement and the novelty of actually *landing* two real fish overcame the exhaustion, but not the absurdity of our predicament.

After congratulating ourselves on our distinguished skills as fishermen, we turned to the next task at hand: getting the hooks out of these toothy creatures and the lines untangled, so we could get back into that school.

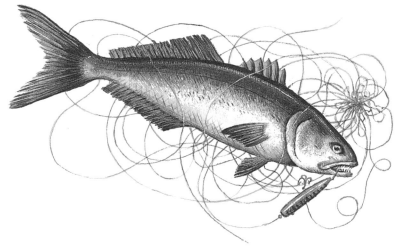

Alan gave the command for me to go aboard *Jedediah* to tend the fish. I ordered him to do the same. After a few seconds of sustained paralysis, we flipped for it. Alan lost. As I tried to keep the now oversailed vessel under control in an increasing wind and sea, he stepped from the afterdeck of *Sazerac* onto the dinghy below. A swell suddenly changed the relative positions of all three, and his foot came down on the rail of the dinghy. Over they went: dinghy, Alan, and two confused fish. The dinghy, port side under, swamped. Alan lurched amidships, somehow righting *Jedediah*. Both emerged from the capsize nearly full of water. Alan had joined the now-replenished bluefish in a very lively seawater bathtub.

The voracious fish now had Alan in their element, rather than he having them in his. The ridiculous spectacle of the situation was exceeded only by the look of alarm on Alan's face. The brown stain at the stern of his khakis gave evidence that the Comfort Factor had vanished as he tried to stand his ground, knee deep in brine, valiantly defending the bow of the dinghy — and his life — with an oar, in a pitching sea, against two slashing, ferocious, and unhappy creatures wielding sharp, triple-ganged hooks. Murphy was clearly a seafaring man!

Suffice it to say, through several acts of heroism, and even more of luck, we won and the blues lost. They were consumed with relish for dinner that night (along with the "long version"). But they did not die in vain, for they bequeathed to us Cruising Rule 15:

 Be careful who you get into a boat with.

16

Captains' Orders

As the bluefish story attests, things happen suddenly at sea. Sometimes a man falls overboard, a keel bumps up on a ledge, a squall makes up. When a crisis erupts, the true sailor immediately and instinctively takes command, displays authority, and exerts leadership. The obvious indicator that this is occurring is the issuance of orders. Many of them. Rapidly. When, however, there are two sailors on board, particularly if co-owners, it is quite likely that each will immediately and instinctively take command, display authority, exert leadership, and give orders. Many of them. Rapidly. It is said that, "We find comfort from those who agree with us, growth from those who do not." Perhaps this is why sailing produces so much growth.

Leadership is one of the most important and least understood of all phenomena. This much we know: for there to be a leader there must be a follower. As you will soon see, when there are two captains aboard, the leadership each inflicts upon the other places both at risk. If it cannot be democratically determined just which partner is the Captain, this could spoil a whole day. Even an entire relationship. Hence the institution of Cruising Rule 16:

 Too many Captains spoil the brine.

We have thus learned that whosoever issues an order is in command. He is to be obeyed unquestioningly. If commands issue from more than one person, they are to be obeyed in the order given.

Nothing welds a knowledgeable, competent sailor to his mate more than being taken seriously, and obeyed immediately. Evidence of compliance must come not only from duty and deference but also from authentic respect. That duo will sail again and again.

17

The Monhegan Meltdown

There's something wholesome, forgiving, innocent, and above all safe about cruising among consenting adults—especially males. Boys' nights on the town are special.

One might then assume that Cruising Rules are universal. However, when man and woman cruise together in relentless intimacy, the situation shifts dramatically, even precipitously— and sometimes perilously.

So it was during one overnight cruise with a member of the opposite sex, when I learned more than I wanted to know about the limitations of Cruising Rules.

One crystal-clear June day, shortly after launching, my friend Petra and I set out for the majestic and mysterious island of Monhegan, twelve miles from the mainland. Petra had never been to Monhegan, and as her guide to Maine cruising grounds as well as her sailing mentor, I was excited to introduce her to this famous landmark for our inaugural "sleepover" aboard ship.

Monhegan's alleged harbor opens to the southwest, receiving unobstructed the prevailing winds and seas of summer. The local fishermen at the lobster pound say that you need seatbelts to stay aboard in that harbor. Uncharacteristic consideration of the Comfort Factor averted the strain to our relationship which this lumpy anchorage would surely have introduced. When we found a mooring over in the lee of the harbor near Inner Duck Rock, a cruise of serene compatibility was assured.

We rowed ashore for a late afternoon walkabout, savoring this lovely island's early-summer flowers and breathtaking views. We returned to our sloop and spent a balmy evening eating garden-grown fare and admiring a beautiful sunset.

Soon a lovely yawl rounded up and dropped anchor beside us where we could thoroughly admire her. As the sun began to set, a quiet moment of romance and solitude washed over us. Lulled by gentle ocean swells and a warm summer breeze, and mindful of her many entangling alliances back home, Petra summed up the moment perfectly: "The great thing about cruising is that those who know *who* we are don't know *where* we are, and those who know *where* we are don't know *who* we are."

My memories of that remarkable evening offer only two foreboding moments: I remember the unusual look on Petra's face as I asked her to rinse the soles of her sandy sneakers before coming aboard—I chose not to inquire of its meaning. Then, supper included Petra's latest attempt at baking zucchini bread, which was a bit weighty. She allowed as it was "good for nothing." I, in turn, offered that we might want to save it. "It might make a good mooring," I said with intent of humor, forgetting

"Good though." Whereupon, another inscrutable look came across her face. Nevertheless, all went well—until we arose from our bunk at sunrise.

We all have our morning rituals which we have followed most of our adult lives. Somewhere along the line, they become what might be called "ingrained habits." Petra, not usually a morning person, *needs* coffee and toast upon rising. I observed her below preparing and buttering a couple of pieces of crunchy rye toast, while liberally broadcasting (I feared) the abrasive crumbs about our living and sleeping quarters. I commented on this behavior and gently and tactfully (I thought) reprimanded her. I suggested that the cockpit with its two generous scupper-disposals was the obvious area for most food on a sailboat.

Breakfast now finished in the cockpit, Petra again went below. I observed her brushing her lovely, long hair—scattering (I feared) blonde strands in cracks and crevices about the cabin, which couldn't be removed until the vacuuming the following spring. I commented upon her behavior and gently and tactfully (I thought) reprimanded her, suggesting she go above to the transom where, I noted, others have brushed for three decades.

Then I jumped overboard to begin *my* morning rituals—relieving myself in the brisk, June, Maine waters by means of what the boys call a "zero-gravity dump." Gasping, I gently, playfully, and tactfully (I thought) invited Petra to join in this morning lustration. She expressed no interest in providing the occupants of the nearby yawl with their day's entertainment by relieving herself in this manner, nor even in jumping overboard and taking a dip.

As I was drying myself with a towel, I observed her brushing her teeth below with our limited fresh water, spattering (I feared) Tom's of Maine all about the cabin. I more strongly and less tactfully (she thought) suggested she stand at the stern, facing aft, and make use, for her morning oral ritual, of the favorable breeze and the inexhaustible supply of seawater.

K-BAM! At that moment our relationship experienced an abrupt sea change. All semblance of intimacy and compatibility vanished. Somehow the series of incidents and gentle and tactful (I thought) reprimands had taken their toll on our budding maritime relationship. Petra exploded in a manner which resembled the sudden, unexpected ignition of gasoline fumes in the bilge. What has come to be called "The Monhegan Meltdown" was out of control.

The next thing I knew, socially saturated, she rowed off in the dinghy with unbrushed hair (and teeth) and a look of fury upon her face which to this day remains indelibly etched upon my retina. When this look recurs (infrequently, thank God), we call it "That Wild Woman of Monhegan Look."

Upon her return some time later, apparently somewhat exorcised, we ventured back to Monhegan and took a short, silent hike to the (now dangerous) high bluff of White Head. Upon our return we immediately set sail, wordlessly, for Round Pond, each occupying a different end of the suddenly very small sloop. Fortunately, the wind, if not the mood, was favorable.

During that interminable sail across Muscongus Bay, I reflected on what had happened. Somehow, my long-comfortable and familiar Cruising Rules had failed. I wondered how I might

put a reef in this woman. Where was her reverence for my intent of humor? Why was the damage suddenly being attributed to "the judgment, or competence, of the individual (me) involved"? What about "Whosoever issues an order is in command and is to be obeyed"? And "The Gods protect sailors and fools"? Only one Cruising Rule seemed to speak to our imperiled condition: "Be careful who you get into a boat with."

A few weeks later when the radiation dissipated, we were able to approach the twisted hulk of The Monhegan Meltdown cautiously. Petra termed my expectations of her, and others, "boat-iquette." Her displeasure with my displeasure with her behavior aboard my boat fell into three categories.

First, I had not made clear the distinction between a request and a rule. These expectations, it turned out, were rules.

Second, these rules were not articulated in a timely fashion, namely beforehand. Consequently, she should be held harmless for all transgressions.

Third, these were dumb rules. Surely few reasonable sailors adhered to such idiosyncratic, obsessive, and controlling ways. (Petra subsequently took a poll—rather biased, I thought—which supported this assertion.)

This story offers us abundant learning and even humor—now: Every Captain has idiosyncrasies. Some are merely peculiar; others are character disorders; and some are downright pathological. They are to be immediately determined and acknowledged. One of several courses of action may then be pursued. A crew member may comply with, violate, resist, ignore, or laugh at the Captain's idiosyncrasies. One may attempt to reeducate the Captain. Or…mutiny.

Oh yes, and the absolutely crucial Cruising Rule 17 emerged, which has enabled Petra and me to enjoy many subsequent, successful overnights at sea—and to keep That Wild Woman of Monhegan bottled up:

 The boy's and girl's night on the town is never— ever—to be confused with the boys' night on the town.

George Washington once wisely observed, "Friendship is a plant of slow growth, and must undergo and withstand the shocks of adversity before it is entitled to the appellation." George Washington never told a lie.

18

The Kids' Night on the Town

Dad, we want to have a slumber party. On *Sazerac.*"
Joanna and Carolyn, my teenaged daughters, had it all figured
out. They and two friends would plan and procure the food for
dinner and breakfast, organize an evening's entertainment, and
perhaps even sleep a bit aboard *Sazerac* at the Round Pond
mooring. I was invited. This was an offer I wanted to, but
couldn't, refuse.

As the early evening mist began to settle in, we rowed out
in *Jedediah* laden with chips, soda, hamburger, catsup, mustard,
M&Ms, radios, sleeping bags, and jammies. Conspicuous by
their absence were zucchini, beer, cheese, and Oreos.

After a few minutes aboard, it became clear that I had dramatically mixed feelings about being a party to this party. On
the one hand, I wanted to be around to supervise the potentially
lethal propane stove and the marine toilet valves (whose improper
use by recent guests had nearly sunk the vessel), and to keep

the hilarity at a level which would not disturb occupants of neighboring vessels. On the other hand, I counted five bodies now packed into the cabin, and four bunks. And I wanted a good night's sleep.

With the kids' unanimous and enthusiastic approval, I decided upon a brilliant plan: one of them would row me to a vacant vessel in the harbor, of which there were many, and I would surreptitiously spend the night on a quiet, albeit unfamiliar deck.

After the stove, the valves, and the hilarity had been tended to, Joanna rowed my air mattress, sleeping bag, poncho, flashlight, toothbrush, nightshirt, and me into the darkness in search of suitable lodging.

Several criteria for the chosen deck quickly emerged. The winning vessel must be out of earshot of the slumber party, it must have six-and-one-half feet of unencumbered deck or cockpit, it must be a sailing craft of some distinction and integrity (why not be choosy?), and it must certainly be unoccupied. There was one moral dilemma: I would prefer to ask for permission. But how to ask if no one is aboard? "Better to ask for forgiveness than permission," says my high school principal friend Tom.

As luck would have it, visiting in port that night, a hundred yards abeam of *Sazerac*, lay a beautiful, wooden, 48-foot Tancook whaler. She offered abundant space on the cockpit counter and was clearly dark and vacant. We came alongside the *Zebra Dun* (should her owner ever read these words, I beseech his forgiveness), and the furtive transfer was made. Joanna rowed *Jedediah* back to *Sazerac* where the party now began in earnest. This was a win-win situation if there ever was one.

I slept very well in the calm summer air, waking only to cast a couple of sleepy glances over to the slumber party to ensure that it was still afloat, and to catch the distant, muffled giggles rolling gently across the water.

In the first light of early dawn, I checked *Sazerac* again. All was in order. She was on the mooring with dinghy tied astern. The slumberers were slumbering, at last. Then, peering out from beneath my sleeping bag and poncho like the beam from a lighthouse groping through the fog, my eye caught sight of something else. Motion in the harbor. To my horror, a dinghy with three people aboard was just leaving the town dock, and heading straight for the *Zebra Dun*.

I had my opening line ready for the owners when they came alongside: "You may wonder what I'm doing sleeping on your boat." But, unable to think of any subsequent lines, I immediately issued—and obeyed—an order to abandon ship. After glancing wistfully at *Sazerac*'s dinghy many yards away, I took the only remaining option. With heart racing, I quickly stripped to the buff, rolled up my sleeping bag, tossed toothbrush, flashlight, and clothes into the poncho, then lowered these provisions onto my air mattress over the side facing away from the oncoming dinghy.

I slid into the frigid water, which seemed even colder than it had the evening before when my bathing suit had been on. "Prune-balls water," Snyder calls it. It certainly gave me abrupt notice that *my* slumber party was over. Like a beaver nosing a poplar branch across a pond, I pushed my raft silently toward *Sazerac* with a new respect for the U.S. Navy SEALS.

In the event I should be noticed and intercepted by the oncoming dinghy, I had another opening line ready: "You may wonder what I'm doing stark naked, pushing an air mattress full of stuff across Round Pond Harbor at six in the morning." But this time I had some better, less culpable supporting lines. Fortunately, I didn't need any of them. With a mixture of sheer terror, numb relief, and hypothermic shivers, I arrived unobserved alongside *Jedediah*. I began to unload my still-dry gear into the dinghy, just as the other dinghy reached the *Zebra Dun*. Whereupon, to my astonishment, I beheld the occupants row right *past* the Tancook whaler and onto the next vessel, which they boarded, completely unmindful of the little drama that had just unfolded.

Later, over a hot cup of coffee aboard *Sazerac* with the now-wakened slumberers, Cruising Rule 19 emerged:

 Before you go to great lengths to extricate yourself from trouble, make sure you're in trouble.

19

She, He, and
the Hurricane

Not long after the slumber party blew through Round Pond, another storm arrived. Gloria was the first major hurricane since 1960 to make landfall in New England. Having dismasted the *USS Constitution*, she left Boston and headed down the Maine coast, carrying with her winds of 120 mph.

LOG ENTRY

27 September, 1985
Round Pond, Maine

0800 hours
Sazerac battened down. Stripped of sails to bare poles. Chafing gear between boat and mooring line. Eerie calm. Flotilla of fishing boats, pleasure craft, and owners wait uneasily. Wondering from which direction storm will hit—and how hard.

1000 hours
Winds picking up. Heavy clouds coming in. Symphony of
halyard strings fills the harbor. Decision: to ride out the storm
aboard *Sazerac* or hold roof on the barn back at the farm?
Choose farm. Row *Jedediah* to town dock; haul her high ashore.
Take one last look.

1500 hours
Sustained hurricane-force winds and rain begin to lash Maine
coast. NOAA weather report from Portland: 75 mph winds
from the southeast. Higher gusts. Tides running four to five feet
above normal. Minimum barometric pressure, 28.50 inches.

1710 hours
Phone rings at farm. Woman in cottage on north side of harbor
reports *Sazerac* dragging mooring through fleet. Missing other
boats — so far. Headed for rocky shore. Battered by five-foot
seas in harbor. End of call. Heart sinks. Helpless. Distraught.

Should have remained aboard to set anchors. Motored ahead
to take load off mooring. Do something. On my watch national
treasure grinds to a horrible end between a wind and a hard
place. Hammered into matchsticks of cedar and oak against
unyielding granite anvil. Guilt. Sadness. Despair. Grief.

Sazerac
1911–1985

1800 hours

Hurricane force winds. Relentless. Farmhouse groans. Phone rings. Unspeakable apprehension. Watchful woman reports *Sazerac* now aground. Working up on ledge at north end of harbor. Listing dangerously to starboard. Heavy seas pound hull. Fearsome winds tear at rigging. Hang up phone. She's done for.

1845 hours

Winds down to 50 mph. Phone rings — again. Darkness at Round Pond Harbor. Tide high. Local lookout reports. Smells diesel smoke. Hears engine. Sees lights. Movement. *Sazerac AFLOAT!* Disbelief. Lobster boat alongside battered sloop. Son attempting rescue of father. A plan. Hope. *Sazerac* being towed off rocks into harbor. Indescribable relief. Wish I could embrace this woman — guardian angel.

28 September, 1985
Head Tide, Maine

0700 hours

Sun up. Wind down. Barn roof intact. Must see *Sazerac.* Arrive at Round Pond, through fifteen miles of downed tree limbs. Fleet rests peacefully at mooring. Brilliant fall maples at water's edge. Find her moored above unfamiliar stone. Dive to inspect hull. Abrasions on stout oak keel. Little damage. Miracle. Retrieve ground tackle from mud. Inspect ledge. Little damage. Seek out rescuers. Protectors of fleet. Discover whereabouts. Hear long version. Learn favorite beverage: Pusser's rum.

29 September, 1985
Round Pond, Maine

1030 hours
Track down case of Pusser's. Deliver fifths to Paul Cunningham, Greg Holmes, Mike Nybo, Mike Prior. Town Fathers, all. Enshrine names in Hall of Fame alongside Henry David Thoreau, Ted Williams, and John F. Kennedy. Row out to *Sazerac*. Sit and stare. Take somber sniff of Pusser's. Contemplate.

Sazerac. Her long journey from master shipwright's hand to rough incarnation fishing for lobsters. Thence to tipsy Southerner's Casco Bay outings. Then lovingly rebuilt atop Bald Mountain in preparation for many more summers squiring families, and zucchini, about Muscongus Bay. And the heroic Outward Bound rescue from the fog off the bony shores of Vinalhaven. And even a proud (if short) participant in the Parade of Tall Ships at Boston's 350th birthday party. How close she came to ending her illustrious career.

How can it be that such ferocious, devastating storms carry the names of the gentler sex? Why indeed, *Mother* Nature?

And I question why any vessel, no matter what the name, is also always a "she." Perhaps so the Captain, seeing her endangered by wind, sea, or rocks, can rush to protect, honor, and love her with the deepest part of his heart and the softest side of his soul? She can make him cry to the heavens, feel unfathomable pain, suffer any indignity—then balm him like no earthly love he has ever known. I drink to her, then to Cruising Rule 19:

A man's love for his boat runs deep.

A man enjoys relationships with the boys, with women, and with children. None, however, resembles his relationship with his vessel. Respect, adoration, tenderness, faithfulness, sensitivity, commitment—love. These are the feelings the Captain experiences toward an inanimate assemblage of wood, brass, bronze, stainless steel, and Dacron—his boat. The reverence with which he fits her out each spring, the pleasure he finds enveloped in her all summer, the attentiveness he lavishes when putting her to bed for the winter each fall, are qualities animate women desperately seek, and deserve from him—yet rarely find.

20

Inside Passage

Several years after the hurricane, and many more good sailing seasons with *Sazerac*, things changed.

A Friendship sloop, although a remarkably accommodating, endearing, and enduring vessel, requires a strong back (there are no winches) and an able crew, especially to raise, handle, and reef the huge mainsail. After twenty-two years and three sloops, I no longer had either. I was reminded of a classified ad I had once seen: "Original owner must sell 22' Catboat. Boat in fine condition; owner showing signs of wear." So, with a mixture of great sadness and realism, *Sazerac* was placed into the hands of a caring steward who had both back and crew. Two years later I encountered a very different kind of sailboat, a 25-foot, full-keeled, Contessa sloop.

Mare's Tail is constructed of fiberglass (yes, I know, "If God had intended there to be fiberglass boats, He would have given us fiberglass trees!") and easily stored and maintained in my barn. But her most practical quality is that she is rigged with a roller-furling jib and main and can thus be handily sailed—alone.

Mariners have always dreamed of facing the winds and waves alone. Many have. Joshua Slocum, in 1896, was the first to solo-circumnavigate the globe. And, it turns out, two of the most recent sailors to accomplish this remarkable feat—both the youngest woman and the youngest man—sailed a Contessa.

Whether around the world, around the Horn, or around the bay, there is something profoundly different about sailing singlehanded. For, when one goes it alone, he comes up against another relationship—the relationship with himself.

Recently, I sailed from Muscongus Bay to visit a good friend on Isle au Haut, on what became an adventure of a different sort. The first day out offered ample distractions which held my thoughts "out there"—tacking, navigating, dodging pot buoys, preparing and eating meals. Just before nightfall, I picked up a guest mooring off Lookout Point and removed the lifeline which, all day, had kept me safely harnessed to *Mare's Tail*.

Gordie rowed out to greet me in *Wilbur*, his venerable dinghy—a cold beer for me seated on the stern. We enjoyed a fine Isle au Haut dinner complete with hamburgers (his) and zucchini (mine). The next morning, after a good sleep on their guest mooring, I rowed ashore to explore the bumpy roads of this raw and remote island with him. Good truck. Bad roads. Good company. Spectacular island. By noon, with tide falling and wind rising, it was time to return to Muscongus Bay.

Mare's Tail and I romped through Fox Islands Thorofare, across West Penobscot Bay, and into Muscle Ridge Channel. As darkness descended, I anchored for the night in a well-protected little bay behind Whitehead Light. Another day of setting out, reaching out, looking out. Another day, out. After preparing and consuming a modest yet imaginative dinner, prominently featuring zucchini, I slept fitfully.

At daybreak, I opened my eyes. At least I *thought* I opened my eyes. Nothing. I saw nothing. Then I knew: Fog. During the night, an unpredicted thick o' fog had smothered Seal Harbor. I could make out my hand but not the bow. Damn!

My impatience to return home and few provisions aboard suggested setting sail. But perilous currents in the Channel, total obscurity, the Comfort Factor, and perhaps a trace of maturity all dictated sitting tight until this veil of cotton lifted. Having weighed the options, I declared for myself what my young daughters used to call a "jammy day," my first in years. Nowhere to go, nothing to see, nothing to do, and nobody to talk with. A day of enforced relaxation.

My jammy day began with reading, occasionally intruded upon by the sound of a gull or muffled lobster boat engine. For awhile, I read a sea story about a father and son sailing around Cape Horn in a boat *Mare's Tail*'s size. But I was having trouble keeping in mind even this gripping tale. Something was stirring within. I was beginning to feel very uneasy out there in the fog—alone. Seeking the comfort of a familiar voice, I turned on the marine radio for the morning weather report. "Widespread fog. Today and tomorrow." What had begun as a welcome aura of relaxation vanished in the fog. I began to feel trapped…with myself.

Like it or not, I guess we are social creatures. A wise theologian reminds us, "Language has created the word *loneliness* to express the pain of being alone and the word *solitude* to express the glory of being alone." For me, solitude had changed to loneliness. I began to talk to myself. Then I invented a companion. To check my position with Loran, I dubbed this navigation instrument "Laura Anne." She gently conversed with me in reassuring numbers. I wished for Snyder, Petra. Even a slumber party.

Then I heard the powerful engine of a fishing trawler growing louder and closer, it seemed. Despite my radar reflector hanging aloft and certainty that my anchor lay in the mud well away from the Channel and passages into the harbor, a doubting voice began to challenge what I *knew* to be true. I wasn't sure now where I was, nor was I sure the other Captain was sure where I was. I began to fear being run over and sunk. I blasted on the foghorn. The sound of the fishing vessel disappeared into the fog. Or had it been there? In my condition of introspection and anxiety, I was experiencing the benefits of what Outward Bound schools call a "solo."

With growing concern, I began to pay close attention to myself and to what was happening to my slumber party. It was becoming clear in that obscure fog that nothing existed except what was in my head. And what was in my head was not comforting. That discomfort seemed somehow familiar. I recalled being lost in the woods, as a five-year-old. I had haunting thoughts of being left and forgotten at a supermarket.

At this point, I would have given the farm for a brisk northwest wind and unlimited visibility. Yet the demons of the fog continued to torment this solitary skipper. I began preparations for dinner and bedtime—at 2:00 p.m. When nighttime mercifully arrived, I sought safety and comfort in my L.L. Bean sleeping bag. I awakened only once to find the stern facing, inexplicably, into the wind. The dream I remembered (or was it a dream?) featured two gigantic lobsters clawing it out on deck until they completely consumed one another. I wondered, had Freud ever gone to sea—alone?

When I awoke in the morning, I immediately peered out the porthole and discerned *land!* A mile visibility. Christopher Columbus could have experienced no greater exhilaration. Within minutes, I was underway. Fog, and my inward-bound experience, soon dissipated as I began, once again, to happily worry about fouling lobster buoys, tide rips, charts, compass headings, and wind directions.

All the way back to Round Pond I contemplated just what kind of companion I am for myself. And, as I thought about my time in the fog confined with myself, I wondered what Cruising Rule might assist a solitary sailor? I had no difficulty appending Cruising Rule 20:

 When you cruise alone, be prepared to navigate the "inside passage."

Upon my return to shore, I shared this "off the chart" experience with Mike, my seagoing neighbor down the hill. He once sailed the Pacific, alone, from San Francisco to Hawaii. Mike claims that sailors fall into two camps. Those who, when given time alone, relish it. Away from others, they do whatever they want, whenever they want, however they want. Those in the other camp, he says, dread their own company and can't tolerate themselves for more than an hour. He told of one skipper, racing alone around the world, who found himself so impossible to live with that he radioed ashore: "Abandoned race to save my soul."

The mind of the solo sailor wanders into very peculiar and disturbing places. Mike reported that one night, halfway to Honolulu, he dreamed—he thought it was a dream—that a weathered old sailor came aboard, took the helm, and altered course back to California. When Mike awoke, the vessel was on an exact compass course for San Francisco Bay. Another single-hander, when asked if he had experienced any hallucinations, reported, "No, they were all real."

When we are alone, the boundary between reality and illusion becomes very foggy. In the fog, the line becomes even foggier.

21

Fair Winds

In Maine, there are two seasons: winter and July. The annual
Columbus Day boys' night on the town notwithstanding, four
months is about all a skipper can squeeze out of the New
England sailing summer—one-third of the year. Yet I know of
no sailor ready to swallow the anchor and hang up his passion
the other two-thirds. Not me. So I have taken a tip from the
noble osprey. I migrate to warmer climates for the winter. At
twenty-five degrees north latitude, southern waters remain in
their liquid state, and sailing can continue.

A few years ago, I found, along the shores of Florida Bay, a
hundred-dollar dwelling on a million-dollar site. Here, an hour
and a half from Miami, I enjoy complete solitude in one of the
least known and most extraordinary sailing grounds in the
world—850 wet, square miles of the Everglades National Park—
provided one's vessel draws less than eight inches.

My winter sloop is a gaff-rigged, 20-foot New Haven sharpie

with leeboards. It is made for these waters. Me too. For in the winter, the winds and bottom are soft, the waters are blue and warm, and the manatee and dolphin are as common as harbor seals in Muscongus Bay. The feeling of exhilaration I experience aboard a graceful sailing vessel breezing across the water on a beam reach, while osprey and gulls wheel and screech overhead, reminds me of summer along the Maine coast.

A sailing vessel is capable of two forms of locomotion: sailing and motoring (not counting drifting a mooring across a harbor

or being trucked to the barn in the fall). A proper sailing vessel always sails.

For many years I believed, "For the sailor without a destination there is no favorable wind; for the sailor with a destination, every wind is favorable." Until recently.

Bob, a very orderly sort, called to invite our friend Jack and me to help move his sailboat from a dock in Key Largo to a new berth on Plantation Key. The plan was to sail the following week down the narrow Intracoastal Waterway in a southwesterly direction. No problem. Almost any wind would get us there — except southwesterly. (Sailboats are great, but their only drawback is an inability to sail directly into the wind — especially into a lot of it.) Prevailing winds during most of the winter in the Florida Keys are east-southeast and north during occasional cold fronts. Never southwest.

When I awoke on the appointed Saturday, my little weather station reported the bad news: a wind direction of 225 degrees — due southwest. Worse news was the anemometer spinning madly at 25–35 knots. The good news? No mosquitoes.

That Saturday brought the strongest and most unrelenting southwesterlies anyone could remember. The boys were forced to motor all the way, under small-craft warnings, getting hammered on the nose for five salty, wet, lumpy hours. The day reminded me of the name I once saw emblazoned on a transom: *Passing Wind*.

The day following our trip, the winds blew favorably from the north, as the day before the trip they had blown favorably from the east. There could be only one possible explanation.

Apparently, the mysterious work of the Town Fathers respects no boundaries. These devils, in their whimsy, rearrange not only navigation aids along the Maine coast but winds along Florida Bay. Clearly, the sailor with a carefully planned destination lives at the mercy of the Town Fathers; the sailor who does not have, or does not disclose, a planned course cannot be confounded by the capricious winds—or Fathers. He confounds Them. Hence, Cruising Rule 21:

 When you declare your intention to sail in a particular direction, the winds will come strong from that direction.

Sailing is an activity best undertaken when you have no need to get anywhere in particular. Bob, Jack, and I agreed that when we *must* sail to a specific place, we will call the others late the night before, at the last moment, when the Town Fathers are abed, and whisper ever so quietly into the phone, "I'm thinking possibly about maybe sailing to Islamorada. Want to come along?"

22

Dismasting the Master

The older I get, the more I need to sail—and the warmer I need to be while doing it. No less of a yachtsman than Juan Ponce de Leon figured out long ago that Florida offers wind, warmth, and water in unlimited quantity. Herein lies his long-sought-after "fountain of youth."

Not surprisingly, friends and relatives from the coast of Maine eagerly leave their wood stoves each winter to stream down to these salt waters, like spawning alewives heading for fresh water in the spring.

My brother Nick and I enjoy an odd relationship, one frequently at odds. Yet we have worked out a variety of treaties which enable us to get along. For instance, each week he drives my trash to the Wiscasset transfer station in his pickup because my back won't permit me to hitch the trailer to my car. But I have to load the trash onto his truck because he can't lift it over the tailgate. He uses my John Deere tractor and supplies all the fuel for both of us. But I have to carry the five-gallon cans of diesel and pour them into the tank. The fact is, we probably have two of the worst backs in the State of Maine, come by honestly, from years of planting and hoeing acres of corn along the banks of the Sheepscot River.

I invited Nick and his wife Sandra to the Keys for a couple of weeks in the February sun to thaw out his ailing back. Shortly before they arrived, I wrenched out *my* aching back. The MRI called it a bulging 4-5 disc. I called it several days of relentless pain, relieved by neither sailing nor swimming. By the time my guests arrived, I was determined to get out on the water and take them for their first sail on Florida Bay. I figured I could lie in state on a cockpit cushion while my crew tended sheets, halyards, and helm. So it was, in this collective condition, we set off one morning under gentle sail and strong medication.

After a balmy beam reach and a leisurely luncheon at anchor off Butternut Key, we headed home to Hammer Point. By then the wind had come up strong. All three of us were now needed as movable ballast to keep the boat upright. Just as I had begun to adjust to the disappearance of my Comfort Factor, a mean gust hit us—*CRACK!* What followed was the third most feared event in any sailor's life (after being swept overboard while sailing alone or gashing a hole in the hull). The unstayed mast broke off clean at the deck, and toppled gently into the sea like the crippled wing of a falling bird.

"Oh dear," said I. A large and unexpected problem. A nightmare in the daytime. So utterly incomprehensible is the dismasting of a sailing vessel that the dictionary in my computer choked on the word. It did offer up, however, some useful alternatives which capture the essence of the moment rather well: "dismantle, dismember, disfigure."

Alas, the drama did not end here. A sailboat without a mast is as useless as a man without a back...and vice versa. Together, their uselessness is compounded. Try fishing out of an agitated bay a mast, boom, gaff, and tangled sail—all laden with sea-water—with two out of three backs aboard decommissioned! Try beating three miles to windward with an undersized outboard in place of a sail. To add insult to injury, run the outboard out of gas, and try to refill it in a pitching sea. And tug and tug on that starter cord with what remains of the crew's dorsal capacity.

All of this did not much improve relations with brother and sister-in-law. It did, however, prepare us for Cruising Rule 22:

 The moment a boat or body part is rendered useless, circumstances will demand its use.

This explains why, when a thick o' fog descended over Easternmost Little Caldwell Island in Maine last summer, and I desperately fumbled for the manual speed indicator, the very finger I needed to punch the key of the Loran was the bloody one I had sliced in the locker clasp.

A skipper with a broken-down back, wrestling with a boat with a broken-down spine, each essential to its most basic functioning, suggests just how mysterious is the symbiotic relationship between body and boat.

23

Skinflint Skippers

Hlow much did it cost?" the guest inquired, admiring J. P. Morgan's 300-foot yacht, *Corsair*.

"If you have to ask, you can't afford one," replied Mr. Morgan.

Countless others have since pondered the connection between boats and dollars.

Ever since we met at age fifteen, Gordon and I have been friendly competitors—beginning with our Model A Fords. Whose was in best shape? Whose restoration was superior? Whose classic automobile was most attractive to the girl with whom we were both infatuated?

In more recent times, Gordon has taken up sailing. In but a few years his vessels jumped from 16 feet to 26 feet to 30 feet. He was a goner. Quite naturally, Gordon and I began to compete about sailing. Not, as one might suppose, in boat length, speed, class, or even beauty. You see, Gordon, married to a Scottish lass, is a very frugal person. I am a parsimonious Yankee. It was only natural that our competition in boats would have to do with money. Our continuing midlife duel is not over who spends the *most* but who spends the *least* on his insatiable sailing habit.

Our calculations are not based simply upon annual yard bills, insurance premiums, or new equipment. Gordon, a shrewd businessman, insists that the only proper standard for competing is determined by who, at the end of the sailing season, enjoys the most favorable cost-per-sailing-day ratio. Theoretically, one could emerge from a sailing season with each day spent aboard costing ten dollars—say, a $3,300 total expense for 330 sailing days. Theoretically.

In our attempt to minimize The Ratio (and rationalize this expensive habit), we agreed to count days spent aboard even when we never got off the mooring (sleeping aboard to break the July heat spell, for instance) and to count the days our children spent on the boat without us (their night on the town, for instance). We also counted any fragment of a day spent on the boat (driving out to check the automatic bilge pump, for instance).

But ever-increasing costs wreak havoc on tight-fisted Scots and Yankee skippers. For years Gordon and I bantered about The Ratio. We especially enjoyed taunting each other when one of us came aboard to share a sail—thereby reducing the host's cost/sail ratio while the guest was held captive, unable to do the same. Of course, a two or three day cruise worked best of all to cause one's penurious mate to suffer.

I knew The Ratio was getting out of hand when I realized one day, with a fresh breeze up, that I couldn't enjoy working in the garden or tending my bees. I should be out sailing. Nor was

I much looking forward to sailing that summer with Gordon on his boat because of the damage this would inflict on my competitive advantage.

Only once, after hauling for the year, did Gordon and I actually compute our "per unit cost." After carefully considering, and attempting to minimize, all "sailing-related costs" (Must the new roof rack on the car for the dinghy count? After all, it's often used for the bicycle), we each plugged our figures into the calculator, along with our days aboard (which had to be documented in the log).

Unfortunately, that particular season for me had been rainy, foggy, and windless, with a major expenditure on a new rudder-post. After due deliberation, and having withstood each other's demands for an "audit," Gordon's cost-per-day of sailing came out to $510; mine was $570. He won.

But we both lost, since this exercise put a chill on our sailing habits like a cold, October northwesterly. We never repeated it. For, we learned Cruising Rule 23:

 If you have to ask how much it costs, you'll never be able to enjoy it.

Gordon and I continue to taunt one another about The Ratio. But we have resolved that our experiences sailing must be assessed by means other than money: New learnings about seamanship, navigation, self, unforgettable adventures, friendships made and deepened, and new waters explored. The intangibles. Never again will we reduce that which provides nourishment for the soul to dollars and cents. For if we calculate the cost of what we enjoy most in life, we will no longer enjoy it.

24

Thy Will Be Done

Embarking on a cruise, or even a daysail, is an exciting and complex event. Details are crucial: provisions, flotation devices, charts, sleeping bags, zucchini. And timing. If the Captain pronounces that the vessel will depart at 10:00 a.m., guests should arrive at the dock well beforehand. Occasionally, the Captain may arrive first, but under no circumstances must he ever have to wait for a guest's late arrival. Missing the tide or wasting a wind makes the Captain cranky.

But having to be on time at the beginning of a cruise is less important than not having to be on time at the end. No guest should ever come aboard with impending commitments ashore. While at sea, safety, navigation, and sailing the wind, not the obligations of the guests, must be the Captain's priorities. When the concerns of guests are put before the laws of nature, a price will be paid.

Ask Reverend Fred. As a guest on *Sazerac* one weekend, he

insisted on being back ashore to greet his flock by 11:00 a.m. one Sunday morning. Before the sun had risen, we had to vacate a perfectly safe anchorage on an offshore island, set out into a gale,

and sail double-reefed through eight-foot seas across Muscongus Bay to get back to the mainland. The dinghy capsized, we lost the oars, fractured the gaff (again), and we had to tie the pastor into the cockpit with docking lines, as green water broke over the top of the cabin house and the clergyman. Periodically, the good Reverend lost his lunch over the side. Several times we nearly lost him. Reverend Fred still contends that he prayed all the way across and would, in the time-honored tradition, have promised God to build Him a church, if safely delivered, had they not already had a perfectly good one in Portland.

Upon setting foot on land, the vicar—ashen, soaking wet, dehydrated, nauseated, but grateful for my part in his safe deliverance—removed his handsome, dripping bowtie, in which he had left the island clad for worship, and presented it to me in somber supplication. It still adorns my closet door. And every time I see it, it reminds me of Cruising Rule 24:

 Never let anyone on board who has to get off board...for God's sake!

The service commenced at 11:00 a.m. sharp, with Reverend Fred at the helm. To this day, that sermon evokes considerable reflection among the parishioners.

25

Promises, Promises

The parable of Reverend Fred and the troubled waters suggests that the return from a sail is a matter of considerable consequence. If the necessity for an early return dampens the relationships among those aboard ship, the necessity of a late return places the relationships between those aboard and others waiting ashore in peril.

Our complicated culture places too many obligations upon us which pile up, mercilessly, one upon the other. We run breathlessly from one commitment to the next, but somehow it works—most of the time.

I used to set out to sea promising to return for a PTA meeting at 8:00 p.m., a game at Fenway Park at 7:00 p.m., or, heaven forbid, a flight to Cincinnati at 6:00 p.m. "I'll be there!" Sure.

I assembled a powerful armada of truthful and compelling excuses for being late, which, over the years, demolished many a bridge spanning my life at sea with those waiting ashore:

tide came in and stole dinghy from beach

went aground

failure of rigging

hadn't finished Long Version

took longer than expected to apply cat's-ass brindle

good fishing

prop hopelessly fouled in lobster buoy, warp, and toggle

becalmed, engine wouldn't start

just becalmed

forgot the Comfort Factor

unexpected wind shift

hurricane

Meltdown

had to improve The Ratio

couldn't get off mooring; couldn't get mooring off

couldn't decide who I was and what to wear

lost the mast

fog

the Town Fathers…

These excuses, no matter how honestly tendered, wore dangerously thin with time, like the threadbare heel of an overused sock. No one ashore seemed to share my amusement in all of this, let alone to understand. For, no matter what the latest in a long line of fascinating causes of delinquency, to be seen as unreliable—to *be* unreliable—is a condition not long tolerated in a relationship.

The truth of the matter is that when you get on, even near, a sailboat, you can't anticipate what is going to happen. Each voyage brings a different surprise. Therefore, it is both impossible and unwise to predict when you will return.

Hence the absolute necessity for Cruising Rule 25:

 When you go to sea, don't promise to return—especially at an agreed-upon time.

I have subsequently found it useful, if somewhat redundant ("Like using a belt and suspenders," Snyder says), to employ the following algebraic formula, and instruct those ashore in its application, as an aid for calculating my *actual* time of return:

$x = 2n + 1$
x = the *actual* number of hours until return
n = the number of hours until *promised* return

Or, if I say I shall be back from the boat in four hours, double that (eight) and add an hour for good measure. Hence, expect me in nine hours. As businessman Alan advises,

"Underpromise and overdeliver."

　　With few promises made, and with the addition of the above "nautical aid," these days there are few time violations, few hard feelings, and the need for few explanations.

The Bourbon Run

"Do you know a cure for me?"

"Yes," he said, "I know a cure for everything. Salt water."

"Salt water?" I asked him.

"Yes," he said, "in one form or the other; sweat, tears or the salt sea."

— Isak Dinesen

The close of many a summer sailing day finds us on a north-easterly course, heading up Muscongus Sound, home to Round Pond. The day's southwesterlies wane as they cross the stern, accompanied by a gentle following sea. Sometimes it's a drifter, sometimes a bit more. With the mainsail fully extended on one side of the hull, and the jib on the other, a sailboat looks like a graceful bird in flight, hence the term "wing 'n' wing." This is a setting sailors call a "run."

As the soft rays of the sun cast warm, orange tones upon the sails, and the trees and rocks ashore, what has been a lively day of beating to windward and heeling is transformed into a timeless—and level—drift downhill. These conditions are favorable for good conversation, reflection, and for a celebratory snort. We call this moment of contentment the Bourbon Run.

These twenty-five rules come from three dozen years of sailing. Let's face it: Relationships are tough. Long-term relationships are tougher. Relations in ships are toughest of all. When you embark on a passage in a sailing vessel—or in a

99

relationship—you will encounter all sorts of surprises and adventures. Don't expect to emerge unchanged.

"The gods do not deduct from our allotted time on Earth the days we spend sailing." Thus it becomes obligatory that each of us spend the maximum number of days at sea. Which, in turn, makes it essential that we find ways to sustain hospitable relationships with our companions, both afloat and ashore.

These rules of cruising have become indispensable for me not only in weathering, but in protecting and enriching friendships during frequent sails on Muscongus and Penobscot bays. Cruising Rules offer to relationships what those in the nation's capital refer to as "diplomatic immunity."

Try them. Refine them. Amend them. Embellish them with the wisdom from your own experiences at sea. Best of all, honor, write, and celebrate your own Cruising Rules—for, each skipper, each vessel, and each relationship demands and deserves its own unique set of rules. But, always bear in mind, while particular Cruising Rules are idiosyncratic and must be reckoned with case by case, the concept of Cruising Rules is universal and immutable.

Nevertheless, as I ponder them, I am struck by their wide applicability. Who knows, if they were broadly adopted, what a wonderfully bonding, balming, and civilizing effect they might have on the workplace, on legislatures, on the crime rate in our society, and on marriages, children, and families. Cruising Rules, like salt water, may well be "a cure for everything."

Now you know why, the moment Snyder comes aboard, he inquires, "Roland, are we on Cruising Rules yet?"

 # Cruising Rules

1   When a party is talking, he is not to be interrupted until he has completed everything he wants to say.

2   Any story worth telling is worth telling often.

3   A statement, joke, or story offered with the intent of humor shall be responded to with audible, visible, persistent, and above all, authentic laughter.

4   Any statement made as fact is, in fact, true and is therefore to be accepted as the truth.

5   Whoever you show up for a cruise as is who you are, and you are to be received accordingly.

6   Non-discussibles may be discussed only within swimming distance of home port.

7   The hand that holds the paintbrush determines the color.

8   That which secures us may also sink us.

9   Whatever is cooked by someone else is to be received, savored, and celebrated with the words "Good though!"

10   The gods protect beginning sailors and fools —
     sometimes both at once.

11   Any damage incurred by a vessel, including fitting out
     at the boatyard, is due to a deficiency in the equipment
     and not to the judgment or competence of the individual
     involved.

12   Reef early and often.

13   Loose lips sink egos.

14   The rightful resting place for every piece of equipment
     on board is at the bottom of the sea.

15   Be careful who you get into a boat with.

16   Too many Captains spoil the brine.

17   The boy's and girl's night on the town is never —
     ever — to be confused with the boys' night on the town.

18   Before you go to great lengths to extricate yourself
     from trouble, make sure you're in trouble.

19   A man's love for his boat runs deep.

20   When you cruise alone, be prepared to navigate the "inside passage."

21   When you declare your intention to sail in a particular direction, the winds will come strong from that direction.

22   The moment a boat or body part is rendered useless, circumstances will demand its use.

23   If you have to ask how much it costs, you'll never be able to enjoy it.

24   Never let anyone on board who has to get off board... for God's sake!

25   When you go to sea, don't promise to return— especially at an agreed-upon time.

Glossary

Adrift: State of locomotion undesirable for a sailboat.

Aground: Where you go if you don't consult the chart; and where, once gone, you never reveal you have been.

Anchor: Piece of ship's equipment designed to sink.

Ashore: Where those who would rather be sailing are.

Buoy: That part of a mooring designed to float.

Captain: He who is always right.

Cat's-ass Brindle: The most beautiful hue in the world.

Chart: What you consult so you won't go aground.

Comfort Factor: That which is to be considered if you want to enjoy sailing.

Command: What the Captain gives.

Crew: They who obey.

Cruise: Two or more days spent continuously on a boat that is underway, with stops for the night.

Cruising Rules: What one must comply with aboard ship to avert interpersonal capsize.

Davy Jones: Keeper of every ship's locker.

Dinghy: (1) Small boat with multiple uses, which may be towed behind a larger vessel if properly secured on a cleat. (2) Container for landing fish—and fishermen. (3) Vessel in which one cruising partner may seek safety when relationship with another is in peril.

Dismasting: Cataclysmic act by which a sailboat is transformed into merely a boat.

Down East: Where people end up, who head Up North.

Esso Map: What you consult if you wish to go aground.

Fatal Attraction: Irresistible urge on the part of ship's equipment to transfer residence from above to below sea level.

Feeling: Unfamiliar equipment members of the male species have but don't know how to use.

Florida: Liquid state in which the sailing water remains all year long.

Head: (1) What you use when you employ the Comfort Factor. (2) What you never employ for comfort.

Laughter: That which enables a relationship to continue.

Meltdown: What happens to a relationship when Cruising Rules are violated.

Mooring: Heavy block of granite, underwater, encrusted with prescription sunglasses, to which a vessel is sometimes secured and by which it may sometimes be sunk.

Motor: That which every proper sailing vessel must have but must never use.

Paint: What the boatyard does.

The Ratio: A number which exists but must never be calculated.

Reef: (1) Reduction in sail area so vessel doesn't go aground. (2) The ground onto which vessel goes if sail area is not reduced.

Relationship: State of tenuous connection between two people, continuously at risk when on a sailing vessel.

Return: What a sailor must never promise to do.

Sailing: Where I'd rather be.

Sink: (1) Stainless compartment into which valuables such as cameras and binoculars may safely be stowed. (2) What a boat does when responding to a holistic Fatal Attraction.

Story: Form of discourse (along with joke and lie) in which it is acceptable to engage while aboard ship.

Town Fathers: The mariner's Greek Chorus.

Trouble: That which you should be sure you're in before swimming nude across a harbor.

Truth: That which the Captain speaks.

Winch Handle: Essential, metallic, elbowlike appliance usually found (or lost) in mud at ocean's bottom.

Wind: (1) Air which passes a sailing vessel propelling it, usually (but not always), forward. (2) Air which passes within a sailing vessel propelling others, usually, away.

Zucchini: Most essential and ubiquitous piece of terrestrial cargo taken to sea.